I0815639

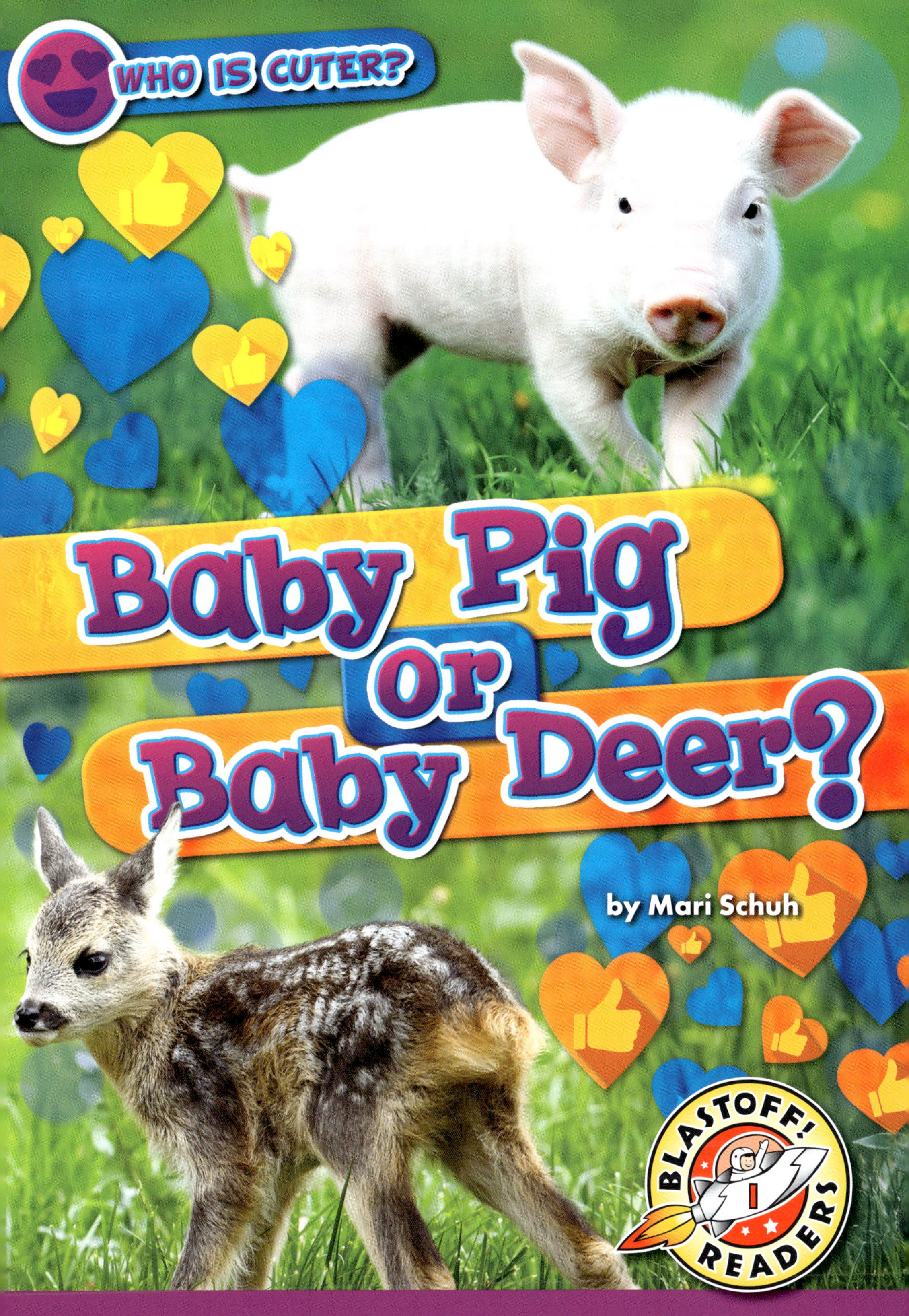

BLASTOFF! READERS: AN IMPRINT OF BELLWETHER MEDIA BY FLUTTERBEE

Blastoff! Readers are carefully developed by literacy experts to build reading stamina and move students toward fluency by combining standards-based content with developmentally appropriate text.

Level 1 provides the most support through repetition of high-frequency words, light text, predictable sentence patterns, and strong visual support.

Level 2 offers early readers a bit more challenge through varied sentences, increased text load, and text-supportive special features.

Level 3 advances early-fluent readers toward fluency through increased text load, less reliance on photos, advancing concepts, longer sentences, and more complex special features.

★ **Blastoff! Universe**

Reading Level

Grade K

Grades 1–3

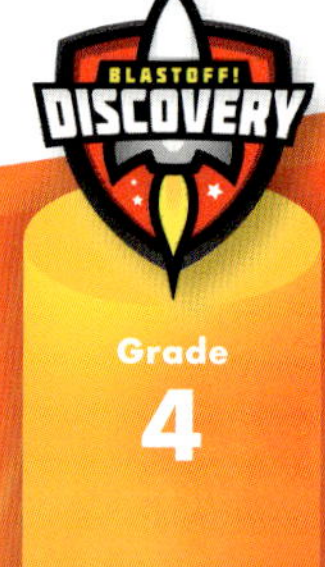

Grade 4

This edition first published in 2026 by Bellwether Media, Inc.

For information regarding permission, write to Bellwether Media, Inc., Attention: Permissions Department, 3500 American Blvd W, Suite 150, Bloomington, MN 55431.

Library of Congress Cataloging-in-Publication Data is available at www.loc.gov or upon request from the publisher.

ISBN: 9798893047745 (hardcover)
ISBN: 9798893048742 (ebook)

Editor: Rachael Barnes

Printed in the United States of America, North Mankato, MN.

Table of Contents

Piglets and Fawns

Baby pigs are called piglets. Baby deer are called fawns.

piglets
fawn

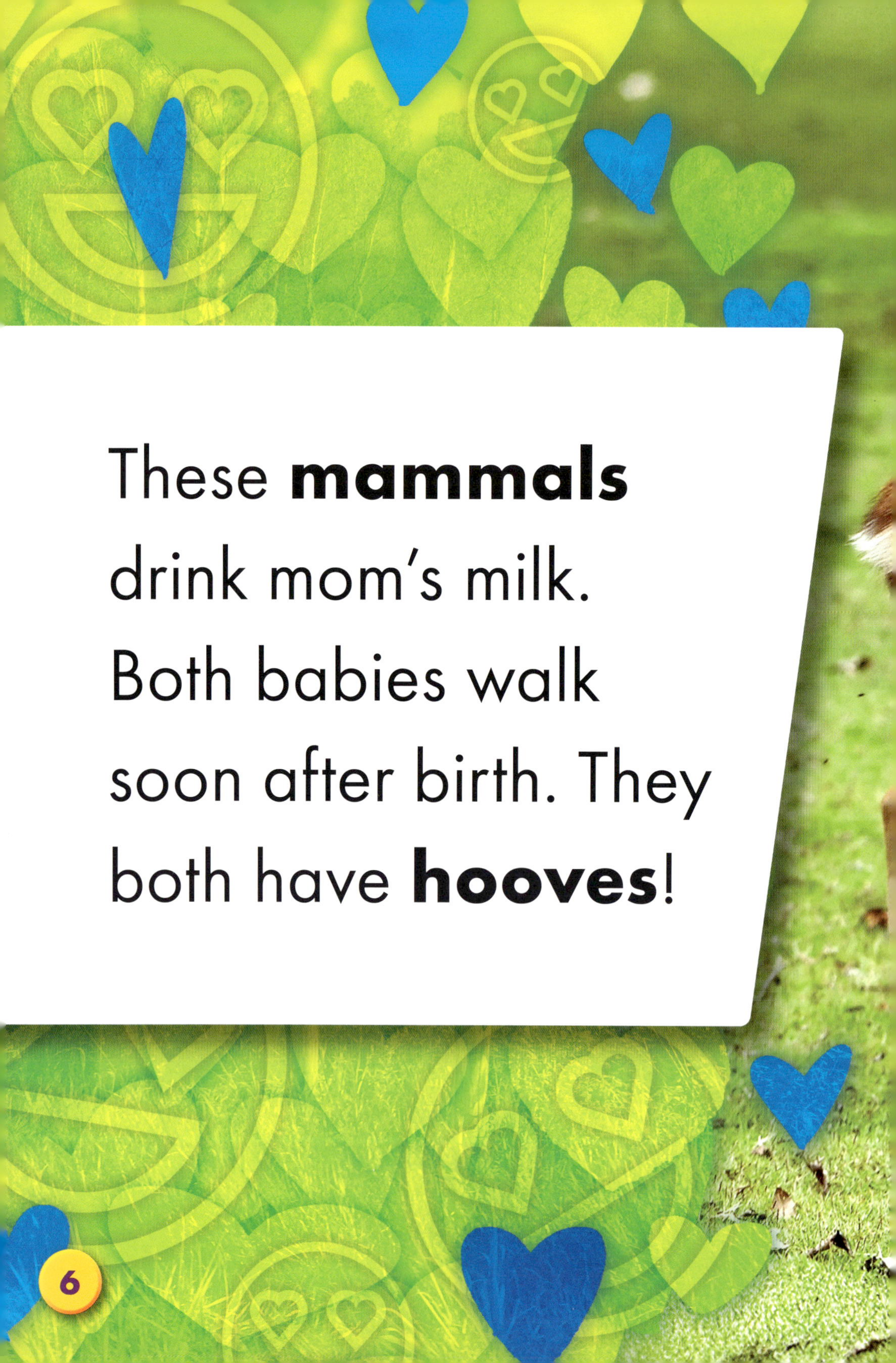

These **mammals** drink mom's milk. Both babies walk soon after birth. They both have **hooves**!

mom
hooves

Noses and Tails

Fawns have long **snouts**. Piglet noses are round and flat.

nose
snout

Many piglets have curly tails. Fawns have furry tails.

curly
tail
furry
tail

Fawns have white spots. Piglets are many colors. Some have spots too!

Growing Up

Fawns are often born as **twins**. Piglets are born in bigger **litters**.

twins
litter

The babies are busy. Piglets dig. Older fawns jump!

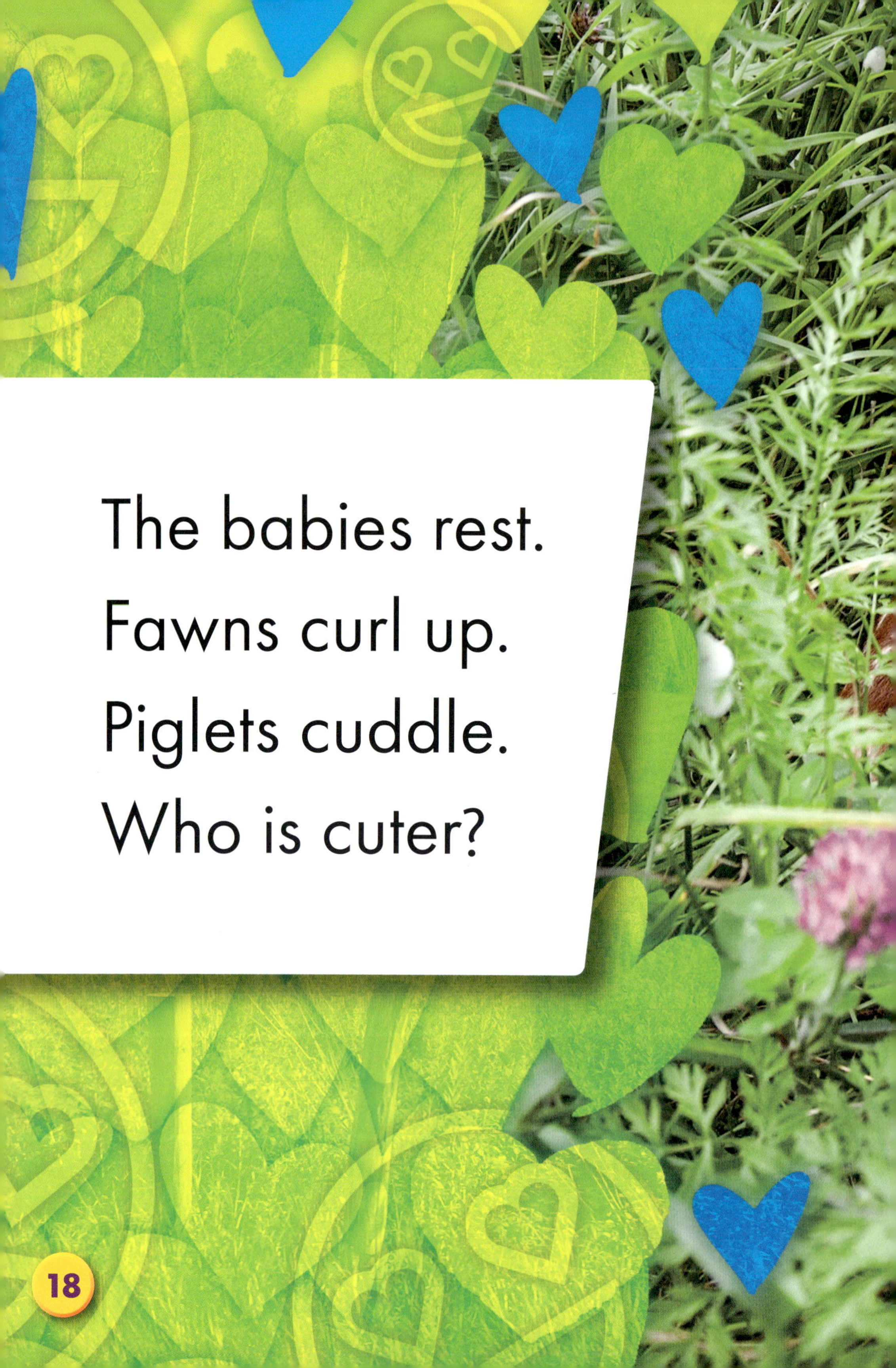

The babies rest.
Fawns curl up.
Piglets cuddle.
Who is cuter?

Who Is Cuter?

curly tail

round, flat nose

many colors

Baby Pig

born in a bigger litter

digs

cuddles

white spots
Who is your pick? Vote at BellwetherMedia.com
long snout
furry tail
Baby Deer
often born as a twin
jumps
curls up

Glossary

hooves

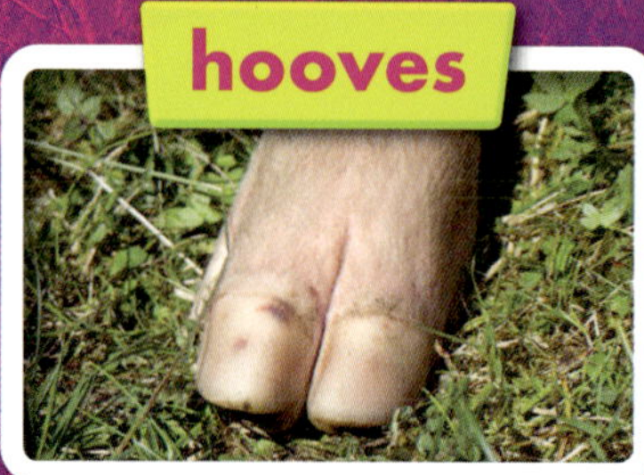

hard coverings on the feet of some animals

snouts

the noses and mouths of some animals

litters

groups of baby animals born at the same time

twins

two babies born at the same time

mammals

warm-blooded animals that have backbones and feed their young milk

To Learn More

AT THE LIBRARY

Arnold, Quinn M. *Pigs*. Mankato, Minn.: Creative Education / Creative Paperbacks, 2026.

Leaf, Christina. *Baby Horse or Baby Cow?* Minneapolis, Minn.: Bellwether Media, 2025.

Morlock, Rachael. *Baby Farm Animals.* Buffalo, N.Y.: PowerKids Press, 2025.

ON THE WEB

FACTSURFER

Factsurfer.com gives you a safe, fun way to find more information.

1. Go to www.factsurfer.com.
2. Enter "baby pig or baby deer" into the search box and click 🔍.
3. Select your book cover to see a list of related content.

Index

The images in this book are reproduced through the courtesy of: Volodymyr Burdiak, front cover (pig); Lubos Chlubny, front cover (deer); Photo Smoothies, front cover (background); Nancy Anderson, background (throughout); Lasse Johansson, background (throughout); amberleigh96, background (throughout); Dieter Kuhn, background (throughout); Galyna, p. 3 (pig); Rehena, p. 3 (deer); Garfield photo2B, pp. 4-5; jared Lloyd/ Getty Images, p. 5; anankkml, pp. 6-7; mikedabell, p. 7; Bigzumi, pp. 8-9; KenCanning, p. 9; Robert Harding Video, pp. 10-11; Elflaco1983, p. 11; new zealand transition/ Getty Images, pp. 12-13; Vera Kuttelvaserova, p. 13; Chris, pp. 14-15; krumanop, p. 15; Anna Perfilova, pp. 16-17; Nina Stavlund/ 500px/ Getty Images, p. 17; Ben, pp. 18-19; iredding01, p. 19; Lanski, p. 20 (pig); markobe, p. 20 (litters); Jonathan_ Densford, p. 20 (digs); Wirestock Creators, p. 20 (cuddles); Willee Cole, p. 21 (deer); Tony Campbell, pp. 21 (twins), 22 (mammals); Joe McDonald, p. 21 (jumps); Sawyers, p. 21 (curls up); Sabine Seiter_sh, p. 22 (hooves); Clara, p. 22 (litters); Andyworks, p. 22 (snouts); Sweet-AZ, p. 22 (twins).